THE
CREATION

THE BIBLE AND ITS STORY

Planned and produced by
Jaca Book–Centurion
from the ideas of
Charles Ehlinger, Hervé Lauriot Prévost,
Pierre Talec, and the editorial committee
of Jaca Book

A chapter outline for this volume
is printed on the last two pages
of the volume.

THE
CREATION

THE BIBLE AND ITS STORY

Text by Enrico Galbiati
Translation by John Shepley
Illustration by Sandro Corsi

Winston Press   430 Oak Grove   Minneapolis, Minnesota   55403

Published in Italy under the title
La Creazione
Copyright ©1981 Jaca Book-Centurion

**Licensed publisher and distributor
of the English-language edition:**
Winston Press, Inc.
430 Oak Grove
Minneapolis, MN   55403
United States of America

Agents:
Canada—
LeDroit/Novalis-Select
135 Nelson Street
Ottawa, Ontario
Canada   K1N 7R4

Australia, New Zealand, New Guinea, Fiji Islands—
Dove Communications Pty. Ltd.
Suite 1   60-64 Railway Road
Blackburn, Victoria   3130
Australia

Acknowledgments:
All Scripture quotations, unless otherwise
indicated, are taken from the *Revised
Standard Version Common Bible*, copyright©
1973 by the Division of Christian Education
of the National Council of the Churches of
Christ in the U.S.A. Used by permission.

All Scripture quotations indicated by *TEV*
(Today's English Version) are from the
Good News Bible - Old Testament: Copyright©
American Bible Society 1976; New Testament:
Copyright© American Bible Society, 1966,
1971, 1976.

Winston Scriptural Consultant:
Catherine Litecky, CSJ
Department of Theology
College of St. Catherine
St. Paul, Minnesota

Winston Staff:
Lois Welshons, Hermann Weinlick - editorial
Reg Sandland, Kathe Wilcoxon - design

Jaca Book-Centurion Editorial Committee:
Maretta Campi, Charles Ehlinger,
Enrico Galbiati, Elio Guerriero, Pierre Talec

Color selection: Mediolanum Color Separations, Milan
Printing: Gorenjski tisk, Kranj, Yugoslavia

Copyright© 1983, English-language edition,
Jaca Book-Centurion. All rights reserved.
Printed in Yugoslavia.

Library of Congress Catalog Card Number: 82-50636

ISBN: 0-86683-191-6

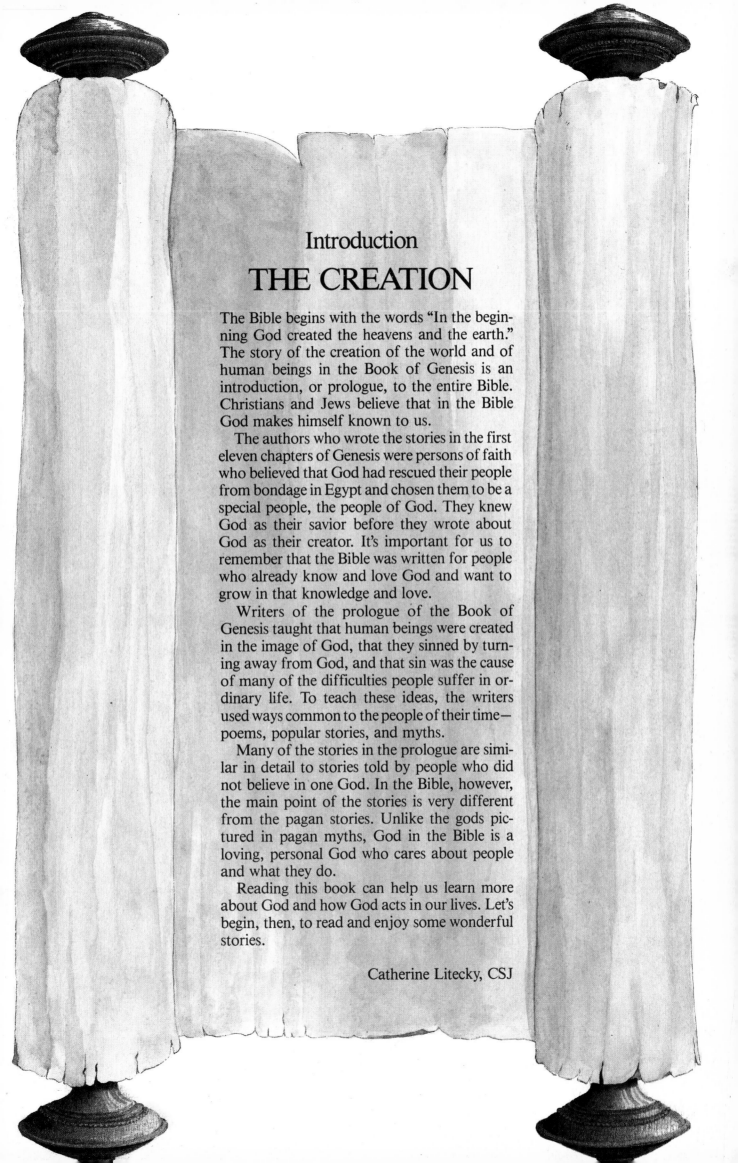

Introduction

THE CREATION

The Bible begins with the words "In the beginning God created the heavens and the earth." The story of the creation of the world and of human beings in the Book of Genesis is an introduction, or prologue, to the entire Bible. Christians and Jews believe that in the Bible God makes himself known to us.

The authors who wrote the stories in the first eleven chapters of Genesis were persons of faith who believed that God had rescued their people from bondage in Egypt and chosen them to be a special people, the people of God. They knew God as their savior before they wrote about God as their creator. It's important for us to remember that the Bible was written for people who already know and love God and want to grow in that knowledge and love.

Writers of the prologue of the Book of Genesis taught that human beings were created in the image of God, that they sinned by turning away from God, and that sin was the cause of many of the difficulties people suffer in ordinary life. To teach these ideas, the writers used ways common to the people of their time— poems, popular stories, and myths.

Many of the stories in the prologue are similar in detail to stories told by people who did not believe in one God. In the Bible, however, the main point of the stories is very different from the pagan stories. Unlike the gods pictured in pagan myths, God in the Bible is a loving, personal God who cares about people and what they do.

Reading this book can help us learn more about God and how God acts in our lives. Let's begin, then, to read and enjoy some wonderful stories.

Catherine Litecky, CSJ

1 All early peoples tried
to explain how the world
and humankind came to exist.
A very ancient poem
called *Enuma elish,*
written in Babylonia, said
that a struggle among gods
was what led to the creation
of the world
and human beings.

How did our world begin? Various peoples in ancient times answered this question in different ways. But in general they all agreed that both the gods and the world had come into existence at the same time through a single process. They believed that the creation of the gods (theogony) and the creation of the world (cosmogony) occurred together.

The Egyptians had a number of theories about the origin of the gods and the world. Their oldest theory said it happened in this way: In the beginning, there existed a vast expanse of water and mud. From this came forth a god which created itself first and then created the earth's surface and other things. Another Egyptian theory about the world's creation said that the god Ptah existed at the beginning. He contained in himself everything needed to form the world. He called into being all the parts of the universe, such as water, earth, and sky. Ptah did this by first thinking of the parts and then saying them aloud.

In Mesopotamia, the homeland of Abraham, the story of the creation was told in a poem known as *Enuma elish,* meaning "when on

high," the words with which the poem begins. ("When on high the sky had not been named, and the earth below had no name....") The poem, written in Babylonia about 1800 B.C., was based on still older stories developed by the Sumerians, who had lived in the area earlier. The poem, which had been written on seven clay tablets, was discovered during the excavation of Nineveh by archeologists in the last century. Here, briefly, is how the poem described the origin of all beings:

Before anything else existed, there was Tiamat, who was an expanse of sea water thought of as a female god, and Apsu, a body of fresh water thought of as a male god. From their union, the first gods were born. They included Anu, god of the sky; Enlil, lord of the air; and Enki, ruler of the earth. From Enki was born Marduk, the special god of Babylonia.

Disturbed by the uproar made by the young gods, Apsu went to war with them, but Enki defeated Apsu, killed him, and from his body formed the lower world, which was an underground sea from which springs of water gushed to form rivers and lakes. Then Tiamat, for revenge, created strange and horrible monsters and placed them under the command of Kingu. Kingu and the monsters prepared for battle to destroy the rebellious gods. Frightened, the gods elected Marduk as their king and protector. Marduk attacked Tiamat directly, killed her, split her in two "like an oyster," and used the upper part of her to form the heavens and home of the gods. Then Marduk created the sun, moon, and stars.

Finally, the gods decided to create human beings. They killed Kingu, Tiamat's helper, and with his blood created human beings, who were meant to be servants of the gods. In this way, evil, which had arisen in the world of the gods, was shifted to humankind, and the gods remained in peace.

2 Most ancient people
were polytheists,
worshipers of many gods.
The Egyptian pharaoh
Akhenaton,
in the fourteenth century B.C.,
was the first important ruler
to insist on the worship
of a single god.
He ordered that this god
be represented by the sun.
After Akhenaton's death,
the Egyptians returned
to polytheism.

Early peoples had rather simple notions about higher beings: There were a supreme god, some good spirits, and other dangerous, or bad, spirits. When the first cities were formed, each city chose its own guardian god. For example, in Egypt, the city of Memphis honored Ptah as its supreme god, while the city of Heliopolis honored the sun god, Re (which some write Ra), and Thebes worshiped Amon.

When, later on, cities grouped together into small states and eventually great empires, the god of the capital city became the supreme god, and the gods of the other cities were organized into families. In this way, a complicated *polytheism* (the worship of many gods) was set up. All the gods were related to one another in various ways. In Egypt, during the New Kingdom, Amon, the god of Thebes, became the country's supreme god because Thebes was the home of the Pharaoh. The gods of Mesopotamia came about in a similar way. Enlil, supreme god of the Sumerians, gave way to Marduk, the god of Babylon, when Babylon became the capital of the first Babylonian dynasty. But all the other gods continued to be honored also.

Monotheism, meaning "the worship of a single God to the exclusion of others," appeared later in the religion of Moses, who taught his people about the one God.

But a century before Moses, the Pharaoh Amenhotep IV (1377–1350 B.C.) had insisted on a kind of monotheism. To Amenhotep, the Egyptian religion seemed to be tied too much to specific places, and he decided that a single God should be worshiped, a God who was not bound to any particular city or country. He believed that this single God was manifested (shown) in the sun, the solar disk, which was called Aton. The sun itself was not worshiped, however. Instead, what was worshiped was the divine force *revealed* in the power of the sun, which preserves life.

Amenhotep IV changed his own name, which means "Amon is satisfied," and insisted on being called Akhenaton, "splendor of the Aton." He then gave up the capital of Thebes, which was connected with the worship of Amon, and built a new royal city called Akhetaton—"Horizon of the Aton." He lived there with his wife, Nefertiti, who supported him in his religious reform, and surrounded himself with officials who had adopted his religious faith. To represent the god, he allowed only the solar disk, with its rays ending in hands (symbols of divine providence) and in a cross with a loop (the symbol of life).

Art, too, was changed by the new religion and became more inspired by nature. The hymn to the Aton wonderfully expresses the Pharaoh's religious ideas: "How numerous are thy works! They are unknowable to man, thou sole God, beyond whom there is no other. Thou hast created the earth to thy desire, when thou wert alone...."

Monotheism in Egypt didn't last long, though. Akhenaton's reform ended with his death, and the pharaohs returned to the old religion with its many gods.

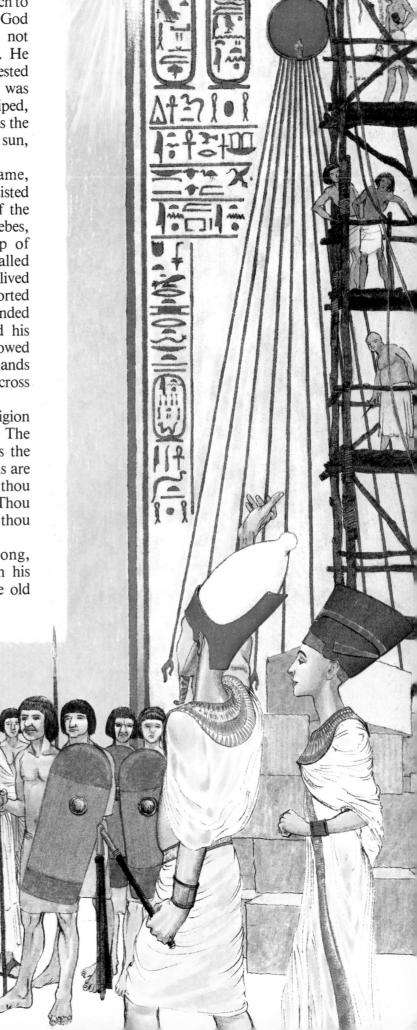

The Book of Genesis, the first book in the Bible, opens with three chapters that tell the story of the creation of the world and humankind. These chapters also tell how our first parents turned away from God.

These creation stories, even though written at different times, have very old roots. They go back to a time when the people who would later become the people of Israel were still only a family of nomads living on the edges of Mesopotamian civilization. Let us look at four moments in the history of the development of these stories, before they became an important part of the Bible.

1) The family of Abraham came from Ur, capital of the last dynasty of the Sumerians. They left Ur and followed the caravan routes going upstream along the banks of the Euphrates River, until they reached the city of

3 The biblical stories
about creation are very old.
The family of Abraham told
stories about creation
that came from Mesopotamia.
Moses changed these stories
so that they presented
the one God as Creator.
Later, scribes of kings
David and Solomon
wrote down the old stories.
Later still, priests in exile
in Babylon again told
the stories in writing.

Haran in northern Mesopotamia. These nomads could not write, but their memories were like storage places from which the ancient stories, including those about creation, were called forth and told and retold to the younger generations. It is not surprising, then, to find that in the Bible's oldest stories there are ideas that come from Mesopotamia.

2) Moses, during the period in which he organized his people in the Sinai Desert after their escape from slavery in Egypt, taught the basic ideas about worshiping only one God. His ideas clashed with parts of the old Mesopotamian stories about creation, and a process of weeding out began. Anything in the old stories that was connected with polytheism was either eliminated or greatly changed.

3) During the reigns of the kings David and Solomon, the scribes and wise men of the court decided to write down the history of the events that had led to the formation of the people of Israel and the kingdom of David. But by now this kingdom was no longer just a cluster of tribes keeping to themselves and concerned only with their own survival. The kingdom was recognized by other peoples, and the scribes of Jerusalem thought they should begin the story of their own people with a sort of history of all humanity preceding the time of Abraham.

To do this, the scribes went back to ancient traditions, stories passed on by their ancestors or picked up through contact with other peoples. They used the stories in order to explain not only the origin of human beings but also the origin of evil, sickness, and death.

These writings, which go from the Creation to the death of Moses, are called the Yahwist writings because in them "Yahweh" is used as the name of God.

4) Centuries after the kingdom of David, during the Babylonian exile, the Jewish priests composed another history about the beginnings of the world, the patriarchs, and the events of Moses and the Exodus. Very likely the authors of what are called the priestly writings knew the Babylonian story of creation. Since they held the same view of the physical world as their pagan neighbors, it is not surprising that they used the same basic outline as the Babylonians to describe the creation of the world.

4 In the priestly writings
about the Creation,
God created the fixed structures
of the universe
in the first three days.
The fixed structures were
light, the sky and the sea,
and the earth
with all its vegetation.

The story of the Creation in the priestly writings was completely free of the two main Babylonian notions about creation. The priestly story did not present the idea that the gods and the world came into being at the same time. Also, the priestly account did not teach that such elements of the universe as the sun, the moon, and the planet Venus were themselves divine beings. Instead, God was said to be the sole creator, with neither competitors nor rivals. God's creations existed as things entirely distinct from God. Creation was meant to serve human beings, who were made in the image of God. Nevertheless, the priestly creation story used Babylonian ideas about the structure of the world—ideas held by the educated people of that time.

The priestly creation story followed a distinct plan and was divided into two parts. In the first part, the structures of the universe that are fixed in place were created (four works in three days). In the second part, the beings that move within the universe were created (another four works in the remaining three days).

Light. In the very beginning, the created world was shown as a mass of earth completely covered with water and wrapped in darkness.

Then God, by a simple command, caused light to exist: God said, "Let there be light," and there was light. Light broke into the never-ending darkness, and light and dark took turns, making the first day.

The sky and sea. God created the sky, or firmament, as ancient peoples pictured it, as an overturned bowl supported by columns. Above the sky was a heavenly sea which had floodgates to allow its waters to fall on the earth in the form of rain or snow. The water on earth formed the sea. This was the work of the second day.

The earth. Dry land emerged from the mass of waters. This dry land, called *earth*, separated from the water, which was called *sea*; each was now distinct from the other.

At God's command, the earth brought forth *vegetation*, classified according to its use by human beings: grass or hay, for cattle; herbs that produce seed, or grasslike plants such as wheat and barley, whose seed helps to nourish people; and trees that bear fruit, each containing the seed proper to its species. (By stating that each fruit tree has its own seed within it, the biblical writers were emphasizing that what existed years later was actually created at the beginning.) Unlike the four works that would next appear in creation, plants neither move, nor fly, nor creep. They are an ornament or production of the dry land, and that's why they were placed with the earth and motionless spaces on the same third day.

Here is the priestly account of the first three days of creation:

In the beginning, when God created the universe, the earth was formless and desolate. The raging ocean that covered everything was engulfed in total darkness, and the power of God was moving over the water. Then God commanded, "Let there be light"—and light appeared. God was pleased with what he saw. Then he separated the light from the darkness, and he named the light "Day" and the darkness "Night." Evening passed and morning came—that was the first day.

Then God commanded, "Let there be a dome to divide the water and to keep it in two separate places"—and it was done. So God made a dome, and it separated the water under it from the water above it. He named the dome "Sky." Evening passed and morning came—that was the second day.

Then God commanded, "Let the water below the sky come together in one place, so that the land will appear"—and it was done. He named the land "Earth," and the water which had come together he named "Sea." And God was pleased with what he saw. Then he commanded, "Let the earth produce all kinds of plants, those that bear grain and those that bear fruit"—and it was done. So the earth produced all kinds of plants, and God was pleased with what he saw. Evening passed and morning came—that was the third day. (Genesis 1:1-13 TEV)

5 In the last three days, God created the moving structures:
the sun, moon, and stars;
the birds and fish;
land animals;
and human beings.

The first four works in creation are usually called *works of separation*. In those works, light was distinguished from darkness, and two spaces — day and night — emerged. The firmament separated two zones containing water — the sky and the sea — another two spaces to be filled. Finally, the rising up of dry land, distinct from the sea, created one more space to be filled — the earth.

In the second part of the story, the ancient priestly author described the filling of these spaces. Inhabitants were placed in the empty places. These were the *works of furnishing adornment*, in which God "furnished" the world.

Sun, moon, and stars. The priestly author wanted to avoid naming the sun and moon, because in Babylonian culture the sun and moon were considered gods. Therefore, he called the sun the "greater light," and the moon the "lesser light." The greater light, moving on high, "ruled" the space of the day; the lesser, together with the stars, ruled the space of the night. Not only was there nothing divine about them, but they were put there to serve human beings. God said, "Let them mark the fixed times, the days and the years, and let them be for lights in the firmament to give light upon the earth." This was the work of the fourth day.

The birds and fish. On the second day, the immense spaces of the sky and seas had been distinguished. Now God made the waters swarm with the living creatures to be found

there, the fish and the sea monsters. And God created the birds, which fly above the earth in the dome of the sky. Then animal life entered the world, and it was to continue by means of procreation. The ancient author said this was according to God's plan, following the blessing, "Be fertile and multiply." This was the work of the fifth day.

The land animals. God's command brought the land animals forth from the earth. They were divided into groups: cattle, which serve people; wild beasts, which live in the forests and on the plains; and "creeping things," all those beasts that crawl or run close to the ground and can become a nuisance or a danger.

Human beings appeared next, as the crowning creation. They entered the world like owners into their own houses, where everything was prepared for them. The importance of human beings was stressed by the solemn tone with which they were introduced: no longer by a simple command, but through a kind of con-sultation within the mind of God. God said, "Let us make human beings in our image, after our likeness."

Human beings had something in them that enabled them to communicate with God and to be in charge of creation: They had the capacity to understand and to desire. At this point, the story sounds like a poem: "God created man in his own image, in the image of God he created him; male and female he created them." The image of God is found not in a single sex, but in both sexes together. Males and females complete one another.

With God's blessing on the sixth day, the work of creation was finished: "Be fertile and multiply; fill all the earth, and subdue it."

On the seventh day, God stopped work. God blessed the day, making it holy because of his rest from labor. The biblical author was suggesting that labor followed by rest is the way human beings should live; after all, God gave us that example.

6 The Yahwist account
of the Creation used symbols
taken from other ancient stories
from Mesopotamia:
the potter who molds clay,
the garden of happiness,
the tree that gives life,
the serpent promising
magic power,
large creatures with wings.

The Yahwist account of the Creation and of the way human beings came to exist made use of objects and images found in ancient Mesopotamian stories. These objects and images became symbols in the Bible story. They stood for ideas the author had about what happened, even though the events couldn't be proven historically. The author, we believe, was inspired by God.

Creation as *the work of the potter*. A potter molds clay and from it creates vases of different shapes and figures of human beings. Mesopotamian myths told about the creator god or goddess forming humankind by shaping clay. Such a procedure also was pictured in an ancient Egyptian painting. The biblical image of God as potter showed that the human body was made from the same elements as the earth's crust. It also presented the idea of a creator who was completely free to shape creatures as he liked.

The garden of God. On the dry plains of Mesopotamia, a garden or orchard—created by human hands and with the help of irrigation—made people think of a wonderful garden inhabited by the gods. This garden image was used in the biblical story to express the original, happy state of humankind. It also was used to show human beings' closeness to God, who enjoyed coming to take a walk in this garden cared for by humans.

The tree of life. This tree had a special meaning in old Mesopotamian stories. It was the tree or plant whose fruit, if eaten, could prolong human life forever; it was the remedy against sickness and death. But people could not have this tree of life, for the gods established death for people and kept life only for themselves. In the biblical story, the tree of life did not grant life that never ends. Rather, the tree of life made it possible to avoid death on the condition of remaining faithful to God. In the Yahwist creation story, the tree of life stood near the tree of the knowledge of good and evil, a tree that God forbade even touching.

The serpent had several meanings in the myths of Mesopotamia. The serpent was either a bearer of good (but a good connected with magic) or a bearer of misfortune. In one myth, the epic of Gilgamesh, the serpent stole the plant of life from the hero. In the biblical story, the serpent was used to tempt human beings, without revealing that he was superior to them and in conflict with God. In addition, the serpent's proposal was connected with magic: eating the fruit would obtain godlike gifts for humans.

In the biblical story, the image of *the cherubim* at the entrance to the garden recalled the winged colossi (gigantic creatures) on the gates of Babylonian and Assyrian temples. Also, the fiery sword at the gate, which threatened anyone trying to get past it was an idea that came from the culture of the ancient Near East.

7 In the Yahwist creation story God, like a potter molding clay, created a man from the earth. Then God gave the man control of a marvelous garden and the creatures in it. In the garden was a tree with fruit that the man was forbidden to eat. Finally, God created a woman. The man and the woman trusted and loved each other.

The Yahwist story of the Creation followed a plan different from the priestly story. In the Yahwist story, when God created the sky and earth, vegetation did not yet exist. First God formed a man from the "clay of the ground"— this was the image of the potter. And this powerful potter was able to blow the breath of life into the nostrils of the man and make him become a being who breathes and has life. What was expressed here was not the idea of body and soul, but rather the idea that what gives life to human beings doesn't come from the earth but from God's creative strength.

And the Lord God planted a garden in Eden, in the east; and there he put the man whom he had formed. And out of the ground the Lord God made to grow every tree that is pleasant to the sight and good for food, the tree of life also in the midst of the garden, and the tree of the knowledge of good and

evil. . . . The Lord God took the man and put him in the garden of Eden to till it and keep it. And the Lord God commanded the man, saying, "You may freely eat of every tree of the garden; but of the tree of the knowledge of good and evil you shall not eat, for in the day that you eat of it you shall die."

(Genesis 2:8-9, 15-17)

Next, God, again in the image of a potter, formed animals and birds from the earth. The man, who was lonely, reviewed all the animals and gave them appropriate names. (The man's act of giving each animal a name meant that he had control over it.) But the man was still feeling very alone.

God, in creating a companion for the man, acted like a surgeon, according to the story's author. From the side of the sleeping man, God took a rib (symbol of life), formed the woman from it, and showed her to the man. Awaken-

ing as from a dream, the man recognized who it was: "This one, at last, is bone of my bones and flesh of my flesh." He gave her the appropriate name woman, *ishsha*, meaning "from man." The author used this creation scene to explain the union of marriage. He said, "That is why a man leaves his father and mother and is united with his wife, and they become one" (Genesis 2:24 TEV). Later on, Jesus explained this passage by using it to support monogamy (the marriage of one man and one woman) and the idea that marriage should be permanent.

Finally, the Yahwist author said that the man and woman though naked were not ashamed. In saying that, he seemed to stress that they trusted one another completely and did not need to guard themselves.

8 A serpent tempted the woman
to eat the fruit
which God had forbidden.
The serpent promised
that if she did so,
then she would be like God.
Both the woman and the man
disobeyed God
and ate the forbidden fruit.

According to the Yahwist writer, the peace and happiness present at the beginning of creation came to an end in the story of the temptation and the sin of the man and the woman. In the story, the writer pictured temptation as coming from creation itself. It came from the serpent, who symbolized the power both of healing (often by magic) and of secret knowledge which had been forbidden to human beings — knowledge which would give unusual power, strength and fertility. The woman was told that if she followed the serpent's advice she would be like God, "knowing good and evil."

"Knowing good and evil" can mean to know everything. The woman was offered a whole new, exciting way of life, but to gain all this wonderful knowledge she had to disobey God by going beyond what it means to be a creature. The creature was being tempted to try to be equal to God the Creator.

The tree of knowledge of good and evil was a symbol, just as eating of the fruit of the tree was a symbolic action. We do not know the kind of sin that was symbolized. We do know it was a very serious offense. The man and the woman sinned as a result of a temptation. (Later, the Book of Wisdom and the Book of Revelation will reveal that the tempter was Satan, a name that means "the accuser.")

Here is the Bible's account of the temptation:

Now the serpent was more subtle than any other wild creature that the Lord God had made. He said to the woman, "Did God say, 'You shall not eat of any tree of the garden'?" And the woman said to the serpent, "We may eat of the fruit of the trees of the garden; but God said, 'You shall not eat of the fruit of the tree which is in the midst of the garden, neither shall you touch it, lest you die.' " But the serpent said to the woman, "You will not die. For God knows that when you eat of it your eyes will be opened, and you will be like God, knowing good and evil." (Genesis 3:1-5)

In other words, the serpent was saying, "God has told you something that is not true, because he wants to keep you in subjection to him. He is jealous; he wants to be the only one. But you can become like God, despite God, and you can be the creators of your own greatness. Here is the means: the fruit of this tree."

The temptation was directed at the woman. The voice of temptation came from outside, but it was echoed within the woman. And so the disobedience took place. The woman ate the fruit and persuaded the man to eat it, too.

9 Knowing that they had sinned, the man and woman hid from God. God made them leave the garden. He promised future victory over the serpent.

Having eaten the fruit of the forbidden tree, the man and woman waited for the serpent's promise to come true. Instead of their eyes being opened to God's knowledge, however, their eyes were opened to their own nakedness. So they sewed fig leaves together, and made loin-cloths for themselves. Their disobedience to God had broken the beautiful relationship they once had with God and with each other. As soon as they heard the voice of God coming close, they hid themselves in shame.

The Lord God called out to the man, "Where are you?"

He answered, "I heard you in the garden; I was afraid and hid from you, because I was naked."

"Who told you that you were naked?" God asked. "Did you eat the fruit that I told you not to eat?" (Genesis 3:9-11 TEV)

The author of the story was saying that the man was ashamed to appear naked before God because he realized he had sinned.

The man replied to God, "The woman whom you placed here with me — she gave me fruit from the tree, and I ate it." The man's words revealed a new unfriendliness, even hostility, toward the woman.

Then God asked the woman, "Why did you do this thing?" The woman said, "The serpent tricked me, so I ate it."

God then turned to the serpent and, asking no questions, gave a verdict.

The Lord God said to the serpent, "Because you have done this, cursed are you above all cattle, and above all wild animals; upon your belly you shall go, and dust you shall eat all the days of your life." (Genesis 3:14)

Then God cursed the serpent, presenting a glimmer of hope for the future:

"I will put enmity between you and the woman, and between your seed and her seed; he shall bruise your head, and you shall bruise his heel." (Genesis 3:15)

These words are a kind of "gospel before the gospels." They announce the good news of future salvation. Humanity will struggle against evil, but in the end the tempter will be defeated, and the serpent's head will be crushed. The revelation of the New Testament shows Jesus Christ to be the final victor over Satan and evil.

Next came God's verdict against the woman:

To the woman he said, "I will greatly multiply your pain in childbearing; in pain you shall bring forth children, yet your desire shall be for your husband, and he shall rule over you." (Genesis 3:16)

In this story, the author tried to find answers to some very difficult questions: Why is giving birth so painful? Why do men sometimes act selfishly toward women? Why is life so hard at times? Why must people die?

It was sin that was responsible. God had made it clear that the original design had been broken.

Finally, the verdict against the man was given:

And to Adam he said, "Because you have listened to the voice of your wife, and have eaten of the tree of which I commanded you, 'You shall not eat of it,' cursed is the ground because of you; in toil you shall eat of it all the days of your life; thorns and thistles it shall bring forth to you; and you shall eat the plants of the field. In the sweat of your face you shall eat bread till you return to the ground, for out of it you were taken; you are dust, and to dust you shall return."

(Genesis 3:17-19)

Then the first parents were driven from the garden, and the entrance was barred by a flaming sword and two cherubim. But before that, God demonstrated his goodness by seeing to it that the man and woman were clothed in animal skins to protect them against cold and sharp thorns.

10 After the woman and the man
turned away from God,
sin started to affect
all human life.
Many passages of the Bible
describe the results of sin:
worry, fear, restlessness,
violence and quarrels,
the strong hurting the weak,
people without food and clothes.

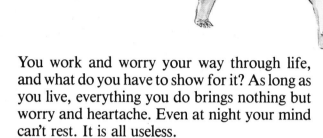

You work and worry your way through life,
and what do you have to show for it? As long as
you live, everything you do brings nothing but
worry and heartache. Even at night your mind
can't rest. It is all useless.

(Ecclesiastes 2:22-23 TEV)

Save me, Lord, from evil men;
  keep me safe from violent men.
They are always plotting evil,
  always stirring up quarrels.
Their tongues are like deadly snakes;
  their words are like a cobra's poison.
Proud men have set a trap for me;
  they have laid their snares,
  and along the path they have
    set traps to catch me.

(Psalm 140:1-3, 5 TEV)

A wicked man does not care about the Lord;
   in his pride he thinks
      that God doesn't matter.
He says to himself, "I will never fail;
   I will never be in trouble."
His speech is filled with curses,
      lies, and threats;
   he is quick to speak hateful, evil words.
He hides himself in the villages,
   waiting to murder innocent people.
He spies on his helpless victims;
   he waits in his hiding place
      like a lion.
He lies in wait for the poor;
   he catches them in his trap
      and drags them away.
The helpless victims lie crushed;
   brute strength has defeated them.
                (Psalm 10:4, 6-10 TEV)

Men move property lines to get more land;
   they steal sheep and put them
      with their own flocks.
They take donkeys that belong to orphans,
   and keep a widow's ox
      till she pays her debts.
They prevent the poor from getting
      their rights
   and force the needy to run and hide.
So the poor, like wild donkeys,
   search for food in the dry wilderness;
      nowhere else can they find food
         for their children.
They have to harvest fields they don't own,
   and gather grapes in wicked men's vineyards.
At night they sleep with nothing
      to cover them,
   nothing to keep them from the cold.
They are drenched by the rain
      that falls on the mountains,
   and they huddle beside the rocks
      for shelter.   (Job 24:2-8 TEV)

11 The man and woman,
Adam and Eve,
had two sons:
Cain, who cultivated the soil,
and Abel, who was a shepherd.
Both brought offerings to God.
Cain thought that
God had been pleased with Abel
but had rejected his offerings.
Cain grew envious
and killed Abel.
This was the first murder.
Cain became a wanderer, but
God protected him from revenge.

After the temptation and sin, the first parents were presented in the biblical story with names — Adam, which means "man," and Eve, which means "life," or "the mother of all living." Adam and Eve had sons and daughters, and the biblical author next told the story of two of their sons — the murderer, Cain, and the brother he kills, Abel. The author told this story in order to show how God and human beings had gotten along in those very early times, and also how human beings had behaved toward one another. In addition, the author told about death's first appearance on earth and about the spread of the first sin.

The names in the story may have come from the traditions of a people called the Cainites, or Kenites, who boasted of descending from a person called Cain. The life of the sons of Adam and Eve was described as if they were living in the Neolithic period, a time when people formed new communities and began to practice agriculture and raise sheep. Farmers and shepherds often found themselves in conflict with each other over land use.

Abel, the Bible said, was a shepherd, and Cain, a farmer, so perhaps they had fights over land. But the real problem between them arose over offerings they made to the Lord:

> After some time Cain brought some of his harvest and gave it as an offering to the Lord. Then Abel brought the first lamb born to one of his sheep, killed it, and gave the best parts of it as an offering. The Lord was pleased with Abel and his offering, but he rejected Cain and his offering.
>
> (Genesis 4:3-5 TEV)

God did not reject Cain's offering because he preferred lambs to the fruits of the earth. How then did Cain come to the conclusion that God liked his brother's offerings and not his own? Probably from the outcome: Abel's affairs had prospered and therefore God must have appreciated Abel's sacrifices, while nothing had

come of his own and so Cain thought God must have been displeased. Cain grew very angry and envious.

In the story, the biblical writer was careful to show that Cain had a choice in the matter. God said to Cain,

"Why are you angry? Why that scowl on your face? If you had done the right thing, you would be smiling; but because you have done evil, sin is crouching at your door. It wants to rule you, but you must overcome it." (Genesis 4:6-7 TEV)

Cain's only reply was to take Abel to a secluded place and kill him.

The Lord asked Cain, "Where is your brother Abel?"

He answered, "I don't know. Am I supposed to take care of my brother?"

Then the Lord said, "Why have you done this terrible thing? Your brother's blood is crying out to me from the ground, like a voice calling for revenge. You are placed under a curse and can no longer farm the soil. It has soaked up your brother's blood as if it had opened its mouth to receive it when you killed him. If you try to grow crops, the soil will not produce anything; you will be a homeless wanderer on the earth."

(Genesis 4:9-12 TEV)

Cain was afraid that if he were off alone, far from the members of his family, anyone would be able to kill him. But the Lord set a mark on Cain so that he would be recognized and anyone who killed him would suffer a punishment seven times greater. And so Cain and his wife departed from the land that for him had become barren and accursed.

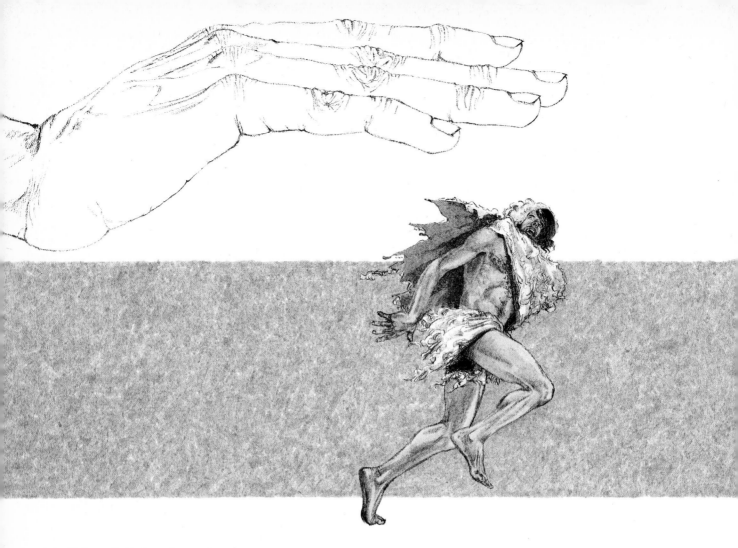

12 The Bible describes
the life and culture
of Cain's descendants —
the first cities,
music,
wealth and herds of livestock,
tools of metal,
pride and violence.
The Bible tells about
Lamech boasting that
he had murdered a man.

Cain fled with his wife to a faraway land. He had a son, Enoch, and built a city for him. Cursed by God but at the same time protected by God, Cain was the beginning of a numerous and warlike people.

In telling about Cain and his descendants, the Yahwist author used the oral history of a people called the Cainites. He also presented that particular history as the origin of all human civilization and progress. The author emphasized that as human beings went further and further away from God, they became more evil and full of pride.

The biblical author next set forth a genealogy, or tracing of a family line. (A genealogy is the biblical way of building a time-bridge from one time period to another. It is important to know that such lists are not meant to be scientific or historical.) In this first biblical genealogy were these names: Enoch, Irad, Mahujael, Methushael, and Lamech. Lamech's sons are credited with a leap forward in human accomplishments. But with Lamech comes the beginning of polygamy, for Lamech marries two women — Adah (meaning "ornament") and Zillah ("little shadow").

Adah's son Jabal was the ancestor of those who dwell in tents and keep cattle. This was the beginning of the raising of livestock on a large scale, which required seasonal moves in order to find vast expanses of grazing land. Property such as cattle meant wealth. And with wealth came leisure time, which allowed the enjoyment of music. Adah's other son, Jubal, was the ancestor of all people who played the harp and the pipe.

Zillah's son, Tubalcain, became an instructor for those who forged instruments of bronze and iron. (Since the people of Cain's time did not have bronze or iron, the Yahwist author had to have been someone who wrote about it years later, when those things were available.)

The Yahwist author by quoting an old song (which Bible scholars later called the "Song of the Sword") demonstrated how extremely

proud and violent Cain's descendants had become. Lamech, in front of his wives, boasted about his murders:

"Adah and Zillah, listen to me:
I have killed a young man
   because he struck me.
If seven lives are taken to pay
   for killing Cain,
Seventy-seven will be taken if
   anyone kills me."

(Genesis 4:23-24 TEV)

God had not approved of revenge against Cain; anyone killing Cain would suffer a punishment seven times greater. Lamech seemed to be saying in his song: "God only went as far as seven times, but I have no need of God; there is someone who will avenge me, not seven times but up to seventy-seven times. Anyone who touches me had better beware!" A Cain "far from God" had led to Lamech, a man "without God"!

13 Adam and Eve had
another son, named Seth.
His descendants were holy
and lived long lives.
Then the descendants of Seth
mixed with descendants of Cain.
Violence and murder
became common.
Strong persons took advantage
of women and weaker persons.

The biblical author gave to the first parents the names Adam and Eve. They were symbolic names. Adam means simply "man," the human being. Adam stood for everything that existed in human beings; both the greatness and the weakness to be found in human beings were present from the beginning. Eve meant "life," referring to women's role in protecting and nourishing children before and after their birth. In other words, Eve was the first mother and the living image of all mothers.

At this point, the biblical writer again said that the first parents had sons and daughters. The emptiness left by Abel's death was filled by another son named Seth; he, too, was dear to God and to his parents.

Then the biblical author once more presented an ancient genealogy. It listed the names that were traditionally given to the very earliest people: Seth, Enosh, Kenan, Mahalalel, Jared, Enoch, Methuselah, Lamech, and Noah. These names may look strange to us, but all of them had a meaning. To indicate that these men were holy, the author attributed very long lives to them. He also pointed out the great holiness of Enoch, whose death was wrapped in mystery: Enoch was taken away by God.

Cain, too, had sons and daughters, but, as we have seen, his descendants were far from God. Intelligent, rich, and powerful, they used their strength to commit violence. Eventually, the wicked descendants of Cain and good descendants of Seth began to mingle, and in that way evil spread. The earth was full of violence! Marriage had become something quite different from what God had intended — no longer were men and women "two in one flesh," united by love for one another. Men had many wives, and the stronger men seized the wives and daughters of the weaker. Murder had become common.

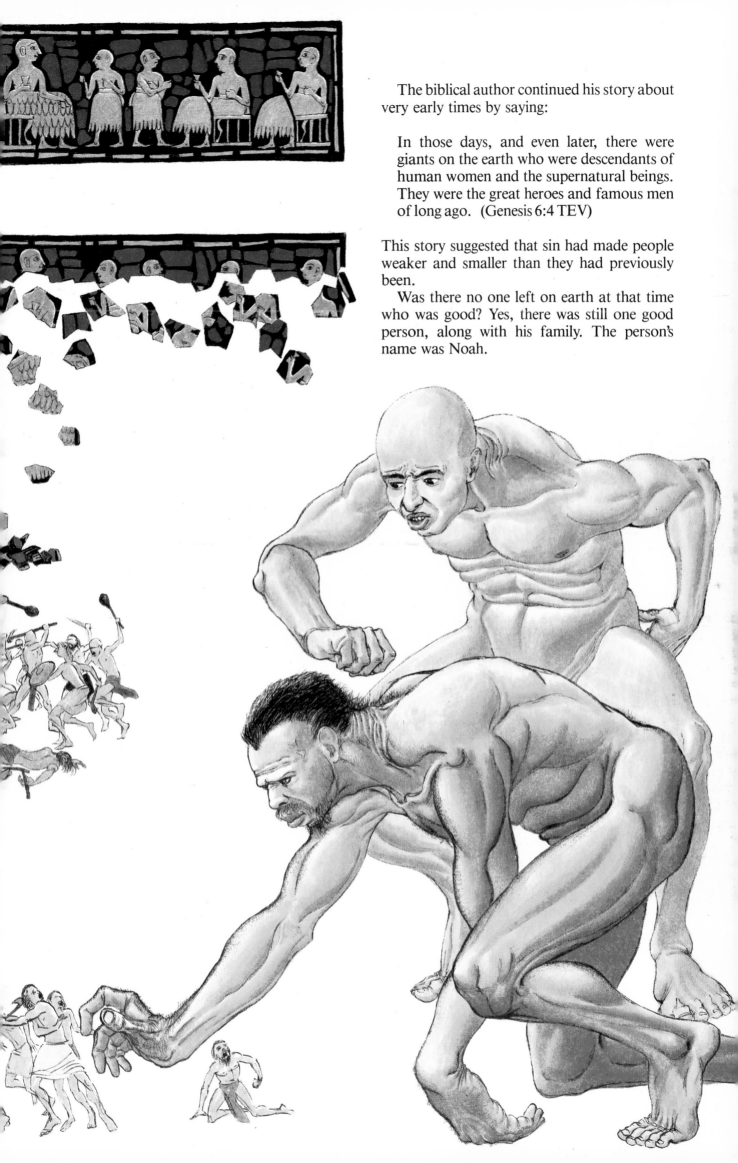

The biblical author continued his story about very early times by saying:

In those days, and even later, there were giants on the earth who were descendants of human women and the supernatural beings. They were the great heroes and famous men of long ago. (Genesis 6:4 TEV)

This story suggested that sin had made people weaker and smaller than they had previously been.

Was there no one left on earth at that time who was good? Yes, there was still one good person, along with his family. The person's name was Noah.

14 Many ancient peoples
told a story
about a flood that destroyed
everyone except a few persons.
A Babylonian poem,
the epic of Gilgamesh,
related how the gods sent
a flood to punish humanity.
The family of Utnapishtim
survived by building a ship.

Even before writing was invented, many peoples were already telling the story of a huge flood that had destroyed all humankind except for one single family or a very small group of people. This story came out of the memory of a disaster occurring so far back in time that specific details about it could no longer be known with much certainty. Instead, the people made up the details of the event.

The Sumerians, the first people to invent writing, also wrote down the story of this flood. They called the flood a deluge, meaning "an overflowing of land by water." Later the Babylonians further developed this deluge story. Luckily, a clay tablet on which the Babylonians had inscribed the story was discovered in the city of Nineveh when it was excavated by archeologists. This story is part of a longer poem which is named after the poem's hero and central figure. It is called the epic of Gilgamesh. The hero of the deluge story, however, is not Gilgamesh but rather one of his ancestors, Utnapishtim, whose name means "he whose life was prolonged."

Here is a summary of this deluge story:

Utnapishtim was the king of Shuruppak, a city located on the Euphrates River. During his reign, the gods — taking the advice of Enlil, "Lord of the air" — decided to send the deluge in

order to punish people for some misdeed. But the god Ea, also known as Enki, "Lord of the earth," loved Utnapishtim and wanted to save him. So that he could say to the other gods that he had not given away their secret, Ea thought up a trick. Instead of speaking directly to Utnapishtim, Ea spoke only to a wall, but behind the wall was Utnapishtim, who heard everything Ea said because the walls of houses were made of reeds. In this way the god Ea informed Utnapishtim that there would soon be a great flood. He advised him to build a square (or round) ship — "equal shall be its width and its length" — and to get on board the ship and save, not only his own life and the lives of his family, but "every seed of life" as well.

Utnapishtim assembled workers, and without telling them the secret, he had the ship built in seven days. Ea gave him a signal that the deluge was about to begin. So Utnapishtim, having entered the ship with his family and every species of animal, pulled up the gangway and closed the hatches.

Then such a terrible storm broke that the gods themselves were frightened: "They fled; they climbed to the heavens of the god Anu; like dogs the gods crouched along the walls." The deluge lasted six days and six nights. On the seventh day the sky became calm, "but all humankind had been changed to mud."

The ship came to rest on Mount Nisir, and seven days later Utnapishtim opened the hatch and released a dove, which soon returned. He then sent out a swallow, which also returned, and finally a raven, which did not return.

Utnapishtim then allowed all his people and animals to leave the ship, and he performed a sacrifice. The gods "smelled the good aroma" and "gathered like flies around the sacrifice." Enlil arrived, saw the survivors, and became angry — his plan to destroy all humankind had failed. Enlil blamed Ea, but Ea scolded Enlil for having caused the deluge to happen. Enlil then took Utnapishtim and his wife, blessed them, and transported them "to the mouth of the rivers," where they lived happily like gods.

15 As the Bible tells the story,
the one God decided to punish
the evil of human beings.
God wanted to save
Noah's family,
because they had been faithful.
God ordered Noah
to build an ark.

The deluge story contained in the epic of Gilgamesh is the most complete and poetic of the flood stories that archeologists have discovered. It was inscribed on clay tablets found later at excavation sites in Assyria and Babylonia. Other stories about a great flood certainly must have existed and been passed down orally. Although differing in some details all of the stories had the same pattern. Certainly

Abraham must have heard some of these stories in Ur and Haran, and it was one of these stories that became the flood story in the Bible.

But while the Bible's flood story follows the familiar pattern, the religious meaning is quite different. In the Bible story, all traces of polytheism (worship of many gods) were kept out of the story. The deluge did not happen because of the whim of one group of gods, opposed by other gods. Instead, the deluge occurred because God, who alone is God, saw the need to destroy wicked humankind and start the story of salvation over again with one good person. The just person was Noah, the last person in the family line of Seth, the third son of Adam and Eve.

Noah's story, along with the story of the deluge, was written by two different authors, the Yahwist writer and the priestly writer. Later, the two accounts of Noah were woven together by an editor. The result was a single, longer account with many repetitions. The two accounts followed the same traditional pattern but had some differences in detail; the editor let these differences remain, and they can still be detected by a careful reader.

In the midst of the great evil in the world, Noah with his one wife and three married sons, Shem, Japheth, and Ham, remained faithful to the Lord. These eight people would be saved from the disaster and would be the new beginning of humanity.

The Bible, in combining the two accounts — the Yahwist one (in which God is called Yahweh, translated "Lord") and the priestly one (in which God is called Elohim, translated "God") — first presents the Lord deciding to bring about the deluge, and then presents God communicating this decision to Noah. The Yahwist account says:

When the Lord saw how wicked everyone on earth was and how evil their thoughts were all the time, he was sorry that he had ever made them and put them on the earth. He

was so filled with regret that he said, "I will wipe out these people I have created, and also the animals and the birds, because I am sorry that I made any of them." But the Lord was pleased with Noah. (Genesis 6:5-8 TEV)

In the priestly version, God tells Noah:

"I have decided to put an end to all mankind. I will destroy them completely, because the world is full of their violent deeds. I am going to send a flood on the earth to destroy every living being. Everything on the earth will die, but I will make a covenant with you."
(Genesis 6:13, 17-18 TEV)

Then God gave Noah instructions for building the ark, and ordered him to enter it before the deluge began, taking with him his family and one pair of each kind of animal.

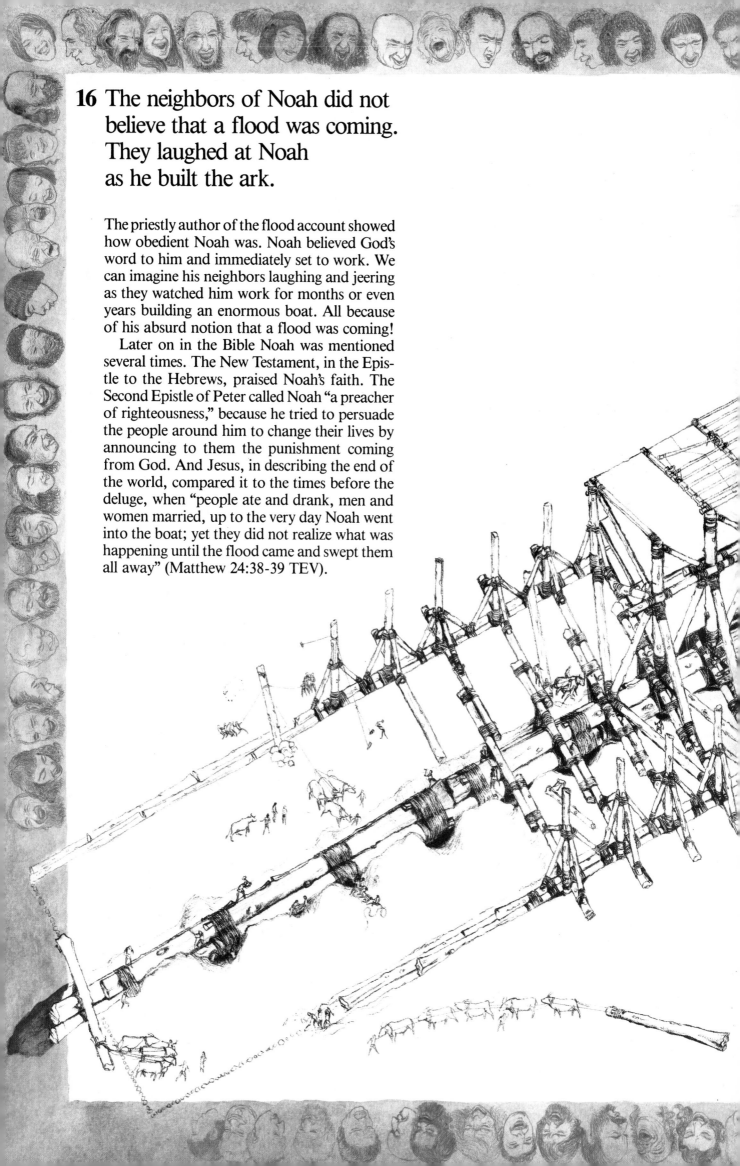

16 The neighbors of Noah did not believe that a flood was coming. They laughed at Noah as he built the ark.

The priestly author of the flood account showed how obedient Noah was. Noah believed God's word to him and immediately set to work. We can imagine his neighbors laughing and jeering as they watched him work for months or even years building an enormous boat. All because of his absurd notion that a flood was coming!

Later on in the Bible Noah was mentioned several times. The New Testament, in the Epistle to the Hebrews, praised Noah's faith. The Second Epistle of Peter called Noah "a preacher of righteousness," because he tried to persuade the people around him to change their lives by announcing to them the punishment coming from God. And Jesus, in describing the end of the world, compared it to the times before the deluge, when "people ate and drank, men and women married, up to the very day Noah went into the boat; yet they did not realize what was happening until the flood came and swept them all away" (Matthew 24:38-39 TEV).

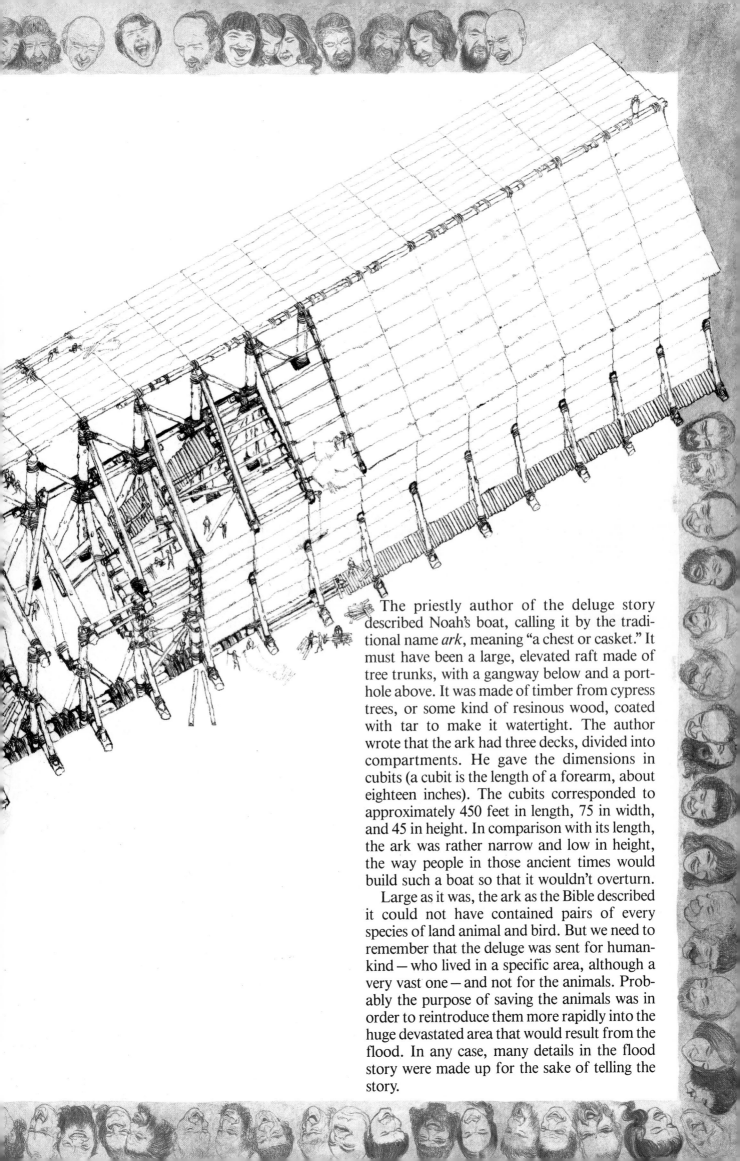

The priestly author of the deluge story described Noah's boat, calling it by the traditional name *ark*, meaning "a chest or casket." It must have been a large, elevated raft made of tree trunks, with a gangway below and a porthole above. It was made of timber from cypress trees, or some kind of resinous wood, coated with tar to make it watertight. The author wrote that the ark had three decks, divided into compartments. He gave the dimensions in cubits (a cubit is the length of a forearm, about eighteen inches). The cubits corresponded to approximately 450 feet in length, 75 in width, and 45 in height. In comparison with its length, the ark was rather narrow and low in height, the way people in those ancient times would build such a boat so that it wouldn't overturn.

Large as it was, the ark as the Bible described it could not have contained pairs of every species of land animal and bird. But we need to remember that the deluge was sent for human-kind — who lived in a specific area, although a very vast one — and not for the animals. Probably the purpose of saving the animals was in order to reintroduce them more rapidly into the huge devastated area that would result from the flood. In any case, many details in the flood story were made up for the sake of telling the story.

17 After the ark was finished,
Noah filled it
with male and female
of every animal species.
Noah's family entered the ark.
Then the deluge began.

We can imagine comments of Noah's neighbors
when they saw Noah constructing his huge raft,
which was not even in a river but propped up on
dry land. Its structure looked more like a
house, or a long wooden building, than a boat
meant for sailing.

In the Babylonian story of the deluge, the
ship was built on the river, and Utnapishtim,
the Babylonian Noah, tried by means of a lie to
keep people from knowing what was going to
happen. At the suggestion of the god Ea, he let
them believe that he intended to emigrate
because Enlil, the god of the country, had
turned against him. During the construction
work, he organized a feast so that no one would
suspect that something serious was about to
take place. Falsehoods like these clashed with
the Bible's idea of God; for this reason, the
Bible story did not include these details.

Once the ark had been built, Noah was
ordered to load it with pairs, male and female,
of all the animal species — beasts, reptiles, and
birds — and food for all of them. According to
the Yahwist account, the Lord gave this order
seven days before the start of the deluge. It

would certainly have taken some time for that whole procession of animals to pass up the single gangway of the ark! The Yahwist account also contained another detail: it distinguished the "pure" (or clean) animals, ones which could be sacrificed and eaten by people, from all the other animals. Noah was ordered to take into the ark seven pairs of each kind of pure animal. The Yahwist account included this detail because later it describes how Noah, after the deluge, made an offering with each kind of pure animal and bird. If only a single pair of each had been preserved in the ark, all the species of animals and birds burned on the altar as a thanksgiving sacrifice would have become extinct!

The priestly writer, on the other hand, did not mention that Noah offered sacrifices because this writer wanted to show that sacrifices were instituted later on by Moses at God's command. So the priestly account simply omitted the incident of Noah's offering, even though a thanksgiving offering surely was part of the ancient flood stories, including the Babylonian version.

The Yahwist story even told how the ark was closed up: When the animals, Noah's family, and Noah himself had entered, "the Lord shut the door behind Noah." The deluge was shown to be the result of direct, steady rain and the sudden rise of the water in the rivers: "All the fountains of the great deep burst forth, and the windows of the heavens were opened." (The word *deep* in the language of the ancient Near East refers to the reserves of underground water, from which gushed springs and rivers.) The water continued to rise, lifted the ark and kept it afloat. People likely tried to escape first by climbing onto rooftops, then by going up into the hills and mountains. But the water kept rising and engulfed them all.

18 The rain stopped,
and the waters went down.
The ark came to rest
on a mountaintop.
Noah waited a while longer;
then all came out onto dry land.
So life on earth
began all over again.

The expanse of water from the deluge covered even the mountaintops, and every breath of life was extinguished on the face of the earth. Only in the ark, that little boat floating between the threatening water and the stormy sky, was there hope for life continuing on earth.

How long did the deluge last? According to the Yahwist tradition, the rain itself lasted for forty days, and then it took three weeks for the waters to recede. According to the priestly account, on the other hand, the water covered the mountains for one hundred and fifty days, then slowly subsided — Noah and his family had to live in the ark for a whole year! As the level of the water fell, so did the ark, until the bottom struck a mountain and the ark came to rest. According to the story, it was a mountain in Ararat, or Armenia, the mountainous region north of Mesopotamia. Then the water con-tinued to recede, while a strong and steady wind speeded the evaporation and draining of the muddy surface of the earth.

The Yahwist account described the end of Noah's stay in the ark:

After forty days Noah opened a window and sent out a raven. It did not come back, but kept flying around until the water was completely gone. Meanwhile, Noah sent out a dove to see if the water had gone down, but since the water still covered all the land, the dove did not find a place to light. It flew back to the boat, and Noah reached out and took it in. He waited another seven days and sent out the dove again. It returned to him in the evening with a fresh olive leaf.

(Genesis 8:6-11 TEV)

Now there could be no doubt. The water had indeed subsided, and vegetation was already beginning to sprout again on the earth. Noah waited another seven days and once again sent out the dove. But when evening came the dove did not reappear, nor did it ever come back. The deluge really was over!

Noah waited for God's order, and only then did he open the door of the ark and allow the living creatures that had been inside for so long to emerge. The animals dispersed themselves over the earth, and flocks of birds flew up into a sky that was once again calm. And so life on earth began all over again, and living creatures multiplied in the vast areas that had been left deserted.

19 The flood story in the Bible
was different from
other flood stories.
It ended with hope,
with the promise
that God still loved humankind.
God pledged never again
to destroy all life.
The rainbow was a reminder
of God's covenant
with humanity.

The conclusion of the biblical deluge story was the part that was the most different from the ancient Mesopotamian flood stories. The Bible story, unlike the other accounts, pointed out very clearly why the flood happened: The flood was God's punishment for the great wickedness that had spread among peoples. The flood was a warning about the seriousness of sin, especially sin that destroys God's plan of order and justice in the world.

But what most distinguished the biblical account from others was the note of hope on which it ended. God still loved humankind, still wanted good for people. The history of the world would go on, and despite people's wickedness, God would lead them to salvation.

The Yahwist version showed Noah and his family, once again on land, offering a sacrifice in thanksgiving to God. Noah erected an altar with a fire at the top and offered up a holocaust (sacrificial victims completely burned) of pure animals and birds — bulls, sheep, goats, doves, and pigeons. The Lord accepted the offering and said:

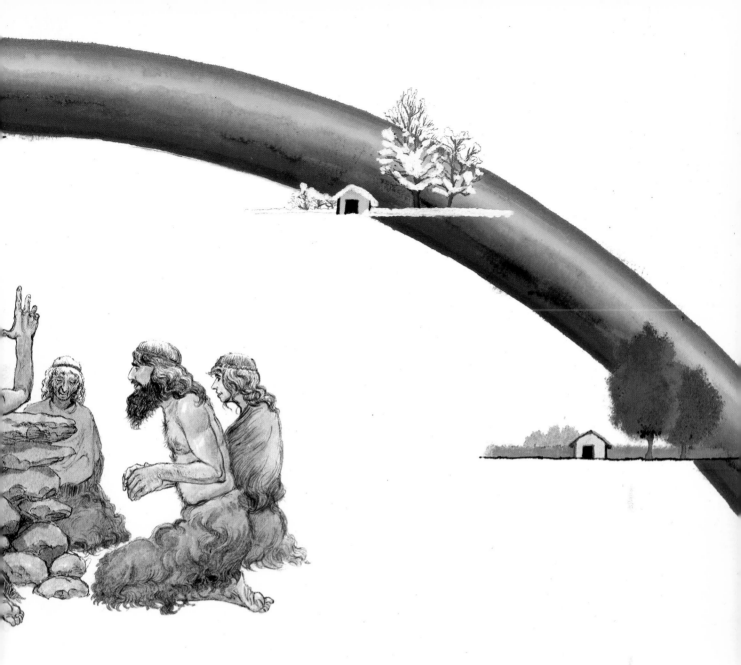

"Never again will I put the earth under a curse because of what man does; I know that from the time he is young his thoughts are evil. Never again will I destroy all living beings, as I have done this time. As long as the world exists, there will be a time for planting and a time for harvest. There will always be cold and heat, summer and winter, day and night." (Genesis 8:21-22 TEV)

The priestly account did not mention the sacrifice, but reported God's blessing, which renewed the blessing given at the beginning of creation.

"Have many children, so that your descendants will live all over the earth. All the animals, birds, and fish will live in fear of you. They are all placed under your power. If anyone takes human life, he will be punished. I will punish with death any animal that takes a human life." (Genesis 9:1-2, 5 TEV)

Then God promised never to send another flood as punishment. God's promise was called a covenant; it was an agreement that God pledged to keep:

"With these words I make my covenant with you: I promise that never again will all living beings be destroyed by a flood; never again will a flood destroy the earth. As a sign of this everlasting covenant which I am making with you and with all living beings, I am putting my bow in the clouds. It will be the sign of my covenant with the world. Whenever I cover the sky with clouds and the rainbow appears, I will remember my promise to you and to all the animals that a flood will never again destroy all living beings."
(Genesis 9:11-15 TEV)

The rainbow, a visible sign of the covenant, appeared in the sky as a symbol of the reconciliation of people with God and as a symbol of the desire for peace among people.

20 One day Noah got drunk and
fell asleep naked in his tent.
Noah's son Ham saw him
and laughed at him,
but his other sons, Shem
and Japheth, covered him.
Noah blessed Shem and Japheth,
but cursed Ham.

The Bible contains a story about Noah that was presented by the Yahwist tradition. The story doesn't seem very important, but its author connected the incident in Noah's life with the religious future of various peoples.

The event in the story unfolds in three parts, like the three acts of a small play. In the first part, Noah worked at cultivating the earth. He discovered how to make wine. One day he became drunk on the wine. While drunk, he took off his clothes and fell asleep naked inside his tent. Though nakedness in the ancient Near East was common among children, slaves, prisoners of war, and the poor in extreme misery, nakedness was considered dishonorable for persons of authority.

One of Noah's three sons, Ham, had very little love for his father. Going into Noah's tent without asking permission, Ham saw his father naked and began to laugh. He went outside to his brothers, Shem and Japheth, and scornfully told them what he had seen. But Shem and Japheth, filled with reverence and compassion for their old father, took a cloak and covered Noah while he slept. As they did so, they walked backwards, so as not to look at their father. In this way, they spared their father the humiliation of being seen by them in his nakedness.

When Noah awoke and found out what had happened, he pronounced a curse on Canaan, who was Ham's son and perhaps his accomplice in the incident. Since Ham, along with the rest of the family, had been blessed by God after the deluge, Noah did not curse him directly, but only indirectly through his son. Noah also pronounced blessings on Shem and Japheth. Noah said:

"A curse on Canaan!
He will be a slave to his brothers.
Give praise to the Lord, the God of
  Shem!
Canaan will be the slave of Shem.

May God cause Japheth to increase!
May his descendants live with the people
  of Shem!
Canaan will be the slave of Japheth."
                    (Genesis 9:25-27 TEV)

Between Shem and Japheth, who were equally honorable, God freely chose Shem. Because of Noah's words, the descendants of Shem (ancestor of the Jews) would have the privilege of preserving the worship of the true God. Japheth (ancestor of the Europeans) was given another, lesser blessing; he would be "increased," meaning that his descendants would be so numerous that they would occupy vast territories. Canaan (the Canaanites, inhabitants of Palestine) would be a servant to both but would not be excluded. Shem, that is to say the Jewish people, would be the custodian of the knowledge of God. Japheth would become Shem's guest ("May his descendants live with the people of Shem"), meaning that the Europeans would receive from the Jews the worship of the true God. Canaan, having become the servant of the Jews, would also be able to learn about the one God. In this way, no one would be excluded from future salvation.

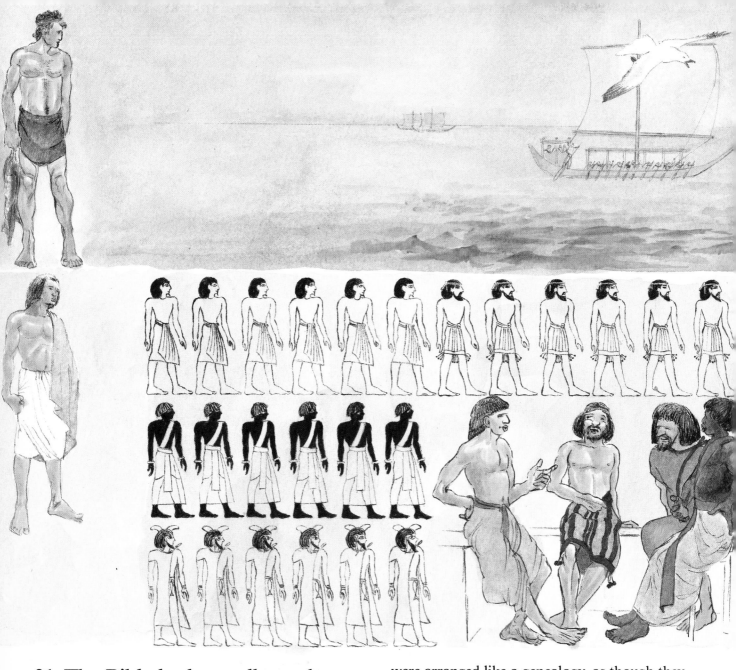

21 The Bible looks at all people as part of one large family.

The Bible teaches that all people are part of the larger family of human beings. To show this, the biblical author of this section presented a geographical listing in which all the peoples known in those ancient times (about seventy) were arranged like a genealogy, as though they had descended from common ancestors.

Certain peoples were indicated by the names of single persons who stand for their most remote ancestors. All these names for peoples were grouped together in three large families that were connected with Noah's three sons: Shem, Japheth, and Ham. But the real reason for grouping certain peoples together was not so much because they were related by blood but because they lived in certain geographical areas.

Japheth's descendants made up the northern populations. They were the Europeans and the

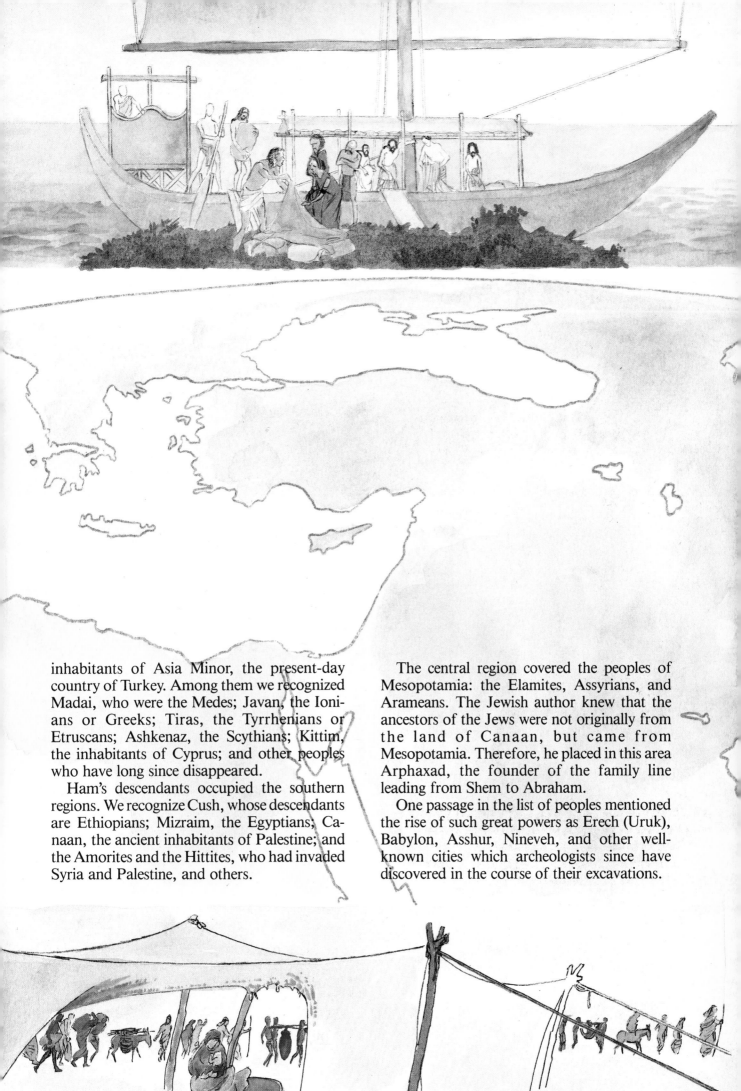

inhabitants of Asia Minor, the present-day country of Turkey. Among them we recognized Madai, who were the Medes; Javan, the Ionians or Greeks; Tiras, the Tyrrhenians or Etruscans; Ashkenaz, the Scythians; Kittim, the inhabitants of Cyprus; and other peoples who have long since disappeared.

Ham's descendants occupied the southern regions. We recognize Cush, whose descendants are Ethiopians; Mizraim, the Egyptians; Canaan, the ancient inhabitants of Palestine; and the Amorites and the Hittites, who had invaded Syria and Palestine, and others.

The central region covered the peoples of Mesopotamia: the Elamites, Assyrians, and Arameans. The Jewish author knew that the ancestors of the Jews were not originally from the land of Canaan, but came from Mesopotamia. Therefore, he placed in this area Arphaxad, the founder of the family line leading from Shem to Abraham.

One passage in the list of peoples mentioned the rise of such great powers as Erech (Uruk), Babylon, Asshur, Nineveh, and other well-known cities which archeologists since have discovered in the course of their excavations.

22 People in ancient Mesopotamia built towers, called ziggurats, as stairways to the sky, where they thought the gods lived.

The Tower of Babel, the subject of a Bible story which is presented in the next chapter, was one of the huge structures that many ancient peoples built in their cities. These structures were not fortified towers for defense, erected, along with city walls, to protect inhabitants from invaders. Instead, these particular tall structures were built for religious reasons. People thought that the towers would be like bridges or stairways between the earth and the sky, where they thought the gods lived.

Even as far back as three thousand years before Jesus, the Sumerians (the founders of Mesopotamia) were building their temples on high embankments so that they would be higher than other buildings. Later on, they began constructing terraces, one on top of another, little by little narrowing the breadth as the height was increased. On the uppermost terrace a small temple would be built.

These structures, called *ziggurats,* were erected in all the main Sumerian cities and were also imitated by the Babylonians and Assyrians. Archeologists have unearthed thirty-four of these sacred towers, in twenty-eight different cities. The most famous one, in Babylon, had seven stories and was called *Etemenanki,* meaning "Foundation House of Heaven and Earth." It measured approximately three hundred feet on each side at the base and three hundred feet

Giza
Memphis
Saqqarah
Medum

Nile

Thebes
Luxor

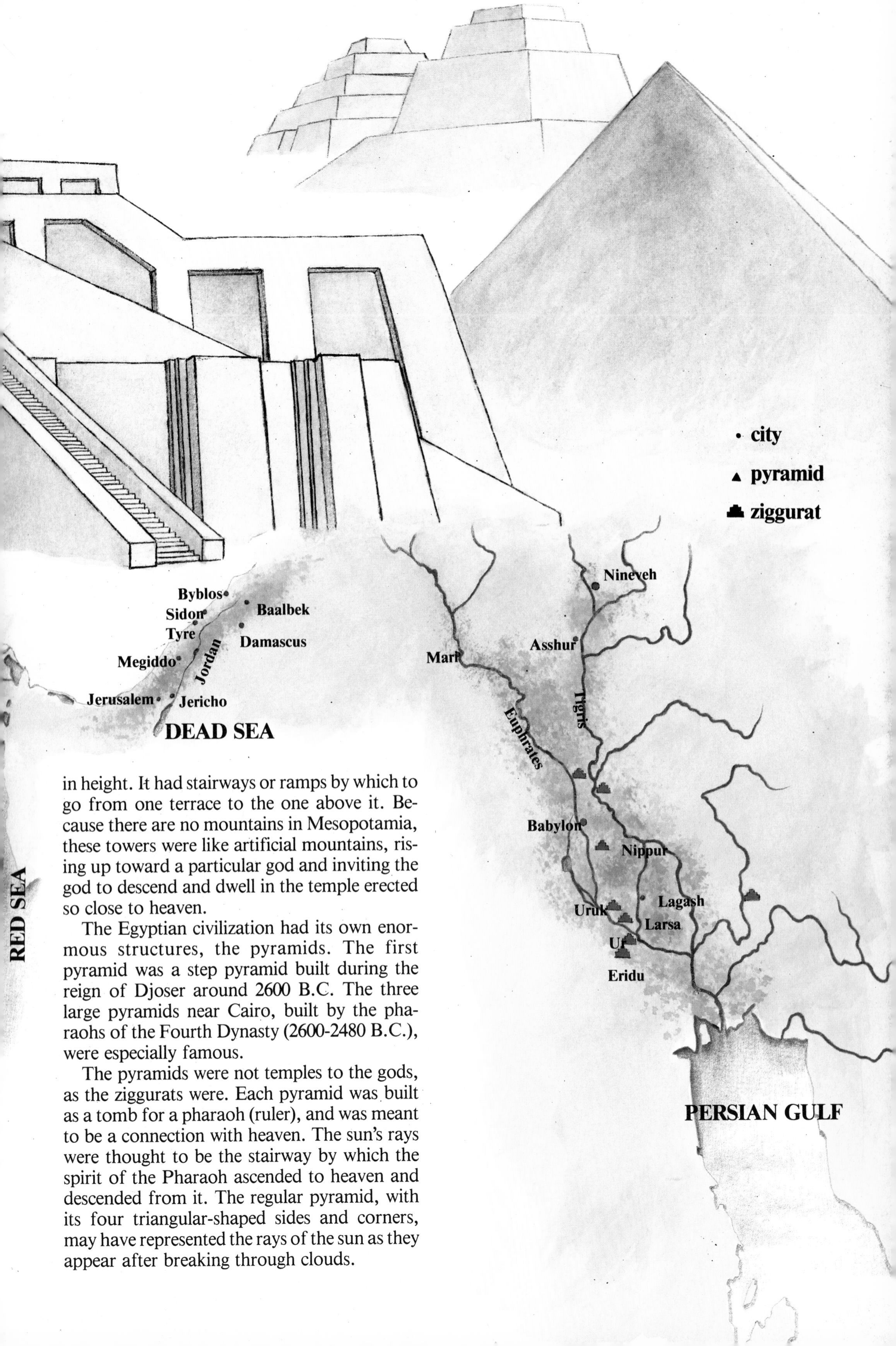

Map labels

- city
- ▲ pyramid
- ▲ ziggurat

Nineveh

Byblos
Sidon
Tyre
Baalbek
Damascus
Megiddo
Jerusalem • Jericho

Mari
Asshur
Euphrates
Tigris

DEAD SEA

Babylon
Nippur
Uruk
Lagash
Larsa
Ur
Eridu

RED SEA

PERSIAN GULF

in height. It had stairways or ramps by which to go from one terrace to the one above it. Because there are no mountains in Mesopotamia, these towers were like artificial mountains, rising up toward a particular god and inviting the god to descend and dwell in the temple erected so close to heaven.

The Egyptian civilization had its own enormous structures, the pyramids. The first pyramid was a step pyramid built during the reign of Djoser around 2600 B.C. The three large pyramids near Cairo, built by the pharaohs of the Fourth Dynasty (2600-2480 B.C.), were especially famous.

The pyramids were not temples to the gods, as the ziggurats were. Each pyramid was built as a tomb for a pharaoh (ruler), and was meant to be a connection with heaven. The sun's rays were thought to be the stairway by which the spirit of the Pharaoh ascended to heaven and descended from it. The regular pyramid, with its four triangular-shaped sides and corners, may have represented the rays of the sun as they appear after breaking through clouds.

23 The Bible tells of the building of one particular tower, at Babel.
The people tried to establish a great empire.
God was displeased and scattered the people by introducing different languages.
This story tried to explain why there were different languages.

The Bible says that Noah's descendants, all speaking one language, multiplied over the earth. They were dwelling on the large plain of Shinar, in southern Mesopotamia, the land of the ancient Sumerians. Here they began to build with fired clay bricks, using tar as mortar. (This information fits with what we have learned from archeological excavations in this area.)

Later these people began building a city with a tower. They said to each other:

"Now let's build a city with a tower that reaches the sky, so that we can make a name for ourselves and not be scattered all over the earth." (Genesis 11:4 TEV)

Saying that they should build a tower that "reaches the sky" was just an expression, of course. What they wanted was a very high tower, visible from all sides, that would be a beacon for the city around which they wished to remain united. In other words, they wanted to establish a great empire.

But the plan of these people did not succeed, for it was not the Lord's plan. The Lord said:

"Now then, these are all one people and they speak one language; this is just the beginning of what they are going to do. Soon they will be able to do anything they want! Let us go down and mix up their language so that they will not understand each other." So the Lord scattered them all over the earth, and they stopped building the city.

(Genesis 11:6-8 TEV)

With a few words, the biblical author had described as one event something that was a slow process — the development of various languages and peoples. In the end, the people, all speaking different languages, found it impossible to remain united. So they separated and scattered over the face of the earth.

The city that was left unfinished was Babel (also called Babylon). The biblical author associated its name with the Hebrew word that meant "confusion," describing it as the place where the confusion of tongues occurred.

This story, which the Yahwist author took from an ancient tradition, contained both some basis in history and a religious lesson. The historical foundation of the story lies in the attitude of distrust and hostility that actually was felt by nomad peoples toward urban centers. The attempt of the Babylonian empire to expand was a real threat to the freedom of the nomads. So when the Babylonian empire fell, both from weaknesses within itself and from the attacks of its neighbors, the nomads rejoiced and spoke sarcastically about their grand plans.

The religious lesson in the story is this: Human unity cannot be created by human armies or governments trying to "make a name" for themselves. It can come only from human awareness that God has made us all members of one family. Against the grand plan of Babel stood Abraham, the nomad not joined to any city or empire. It was to Abraham that God promised, "I will bless you and make your name great. Through you I will bless all the nations on earth."

24 How did the world begin?
Human beings have always tried
to answer this question.
Scientists still try today.
The Bible records the answers
of some people long ago.

In the beginning, God created
the universe.
God, on the other hand,
had no beginning.
God made us to be happy
by loving him and one another.

The Bible opens with these words: "In the beginning God created the heavens and the earth." By "heavens and earth" is meant the whole universe, both what appears before our eyes — like the earth, sun, and stars — and what may be revealed to us by scientific instruments and mathematical calculations. All these things had a beginning. They exist because God made them exist out of nothing; God created them.

God, on the other hand, had no beginning. When the universe began to exist, God existed already. God has always existed. God is eternal. Nothing that can be seen in the universe is God. Everything, without exception, was created by God.

The first chapter of the Bible clearly shows that the universe did not begin in its present form. It tells of God making the universe more and more suitable for living creatures and ultimately for humanity. But even when the Bible uses poetic images, it teaches that God's creative action can neither be known nor described.

Faith in God is not in conflict with science. Science teaches us the nature of matter and energy, and the phases in the development of the universe, but it does not answer the basic question: For what purpose does the universe exist? Faith in God the Creator and Redeemer provides the answer to this question.

According to many scientists,
the universe began long ago
with a great explosion.
From clouds of gas
came galaxies.
Within these were the stars,
one of them our sun.

Between ten and twenty billion years ago, the universe began with a great explosion, a big bang. It has been expanding ever since. At the present time, this is the best scientific explanation of the beginning of the universe.

After the great initial explosion, or big bang, the universe was pure energy and incredible heat. The force of the big bang, which caused a very rapid expansion followed by a swift cooling, led to the emergence of particles of matter, in what might be called a thick soup of matter, radiation, and energy. In the course of this expansion and cooling, some particles combined to form the simplest atoms, those of hydrogen. Then conditions were favorable for hydrogen atoms to merge into more complex atoms, those of helium.

Something like gaseous clouds came to be more and more scattered in space and removed from violent turbulence. In this way, concentrations of matter were formed. After the violent force of the initial explosion was past, the gravitational forces of attraction gained the upper hand. The galaxies, huge collections of matter that behave in a unified way, were thereby born. Within the galaxies, also by the action of gravity, independent bodies, the stars, were formed. Within the stars the temperature again rose. Once more hydrogen atoms merged into helium and other heavier elements. These separated from the stars as independent bodies.

One of these galaxies is the Milky Way. At one end of the Milky Way is the star we call the sun. From the sun, the earth and the other planets were born, receiving from it light and energy. All of the planets together, governed by the force of gravity, rotate around the sun to form the solar system. In the solar system, conditions were favorable for the appearance of oxygen, carbon, and nitrogen. In a watery environment, with just the right elements and the necessary solar energy, small organic molecules arose. These became able to reproduce themselves. And there was life.

25 The Bible and science
in different ways tell how
human beings have come to be.

The Bible says that every form of life has come from God. Human beings, made in God's image, can know and love God.

The Bible does not teach the evolution of species, but neither does it deny it. The Bible states that God created "after their kind" all the creatures in the sea and all the birds, all the creeping things and all the land animals. It does not say anything about *how* God created them but makes it clear that no species of living creature is independent of the creative activity of God. The creative action in itself is not described. Scientists may demonstrate that there has been a process of evolution, as shown by fossils, and that all animal species are like the branches of a tree growing from a single stump — that is to say, from the first and simplest micro-organism. Persons of faith may see that this was the way chosen by God to create the animal world in all its variety.

The same goes for the physical body of the human being. The Bible says that it was made of dust; this means made of the same elements as the material world. But the Bible does not say how. It offers as a comparison — not as a revelation of the mystery of creation — the image of the potter who molds clay. God may have wished to create the human body through progressive evolution from a living being that was not yet human but was meant to become human. This would then be an evolution guided by God, in order to produce a being capable of receiving a soul gifted with intelligence and will.

In any case, evolution involves the body of the human being, not the *whole* person. On this point, the Bible teaches a specific lesson: Humanity is created in God's image and given dominion over the created world. "Created in God's image" means that in some ways humans are like God. Human beings are not just like the other animals, but have souls capable of knowing and loving God. So that humans might fully enjoy this capacity, God has offered humanity the gift of eternal life.

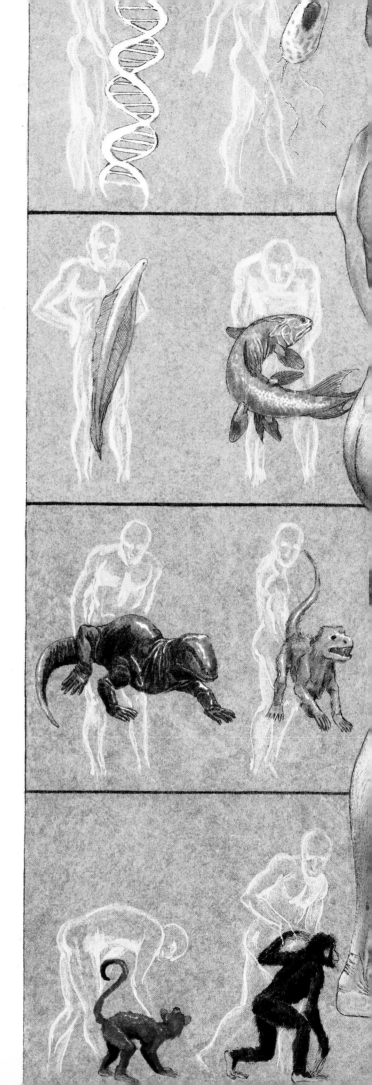

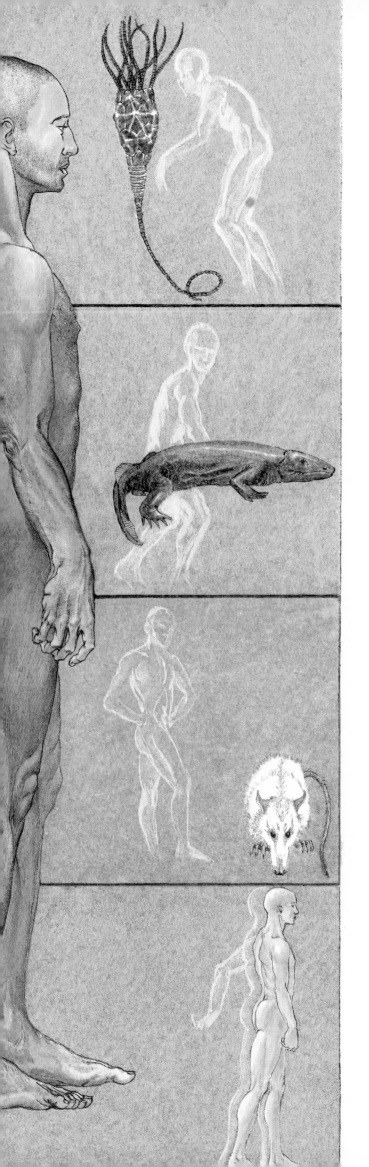

The theory of evolution tells how slowly, over millions of years, complex forms of life have come from very simple forms, and how different species have come from the same ancestors.

Every living body is formed from living cells. In the nucleus of each cell are chromosomes, which contain a very large number of genes. One cell produces another and divides its chromosomes, which leads to a doubling of the genes. The genes contain in themselves all the information to indicate how the second cell, the second living organism, should be constructed from the first. This mechanism of heredity functions in all living beings. This is why children, different as they may be, resemble their parents. When this process of heredity is repeated millions of times, it sometimes happens that unexpected changes occur. These genetic mutations — sudden, bold changes — are then passed on to the children.

The *theory* of evolution presents not only genetic mutation as an explanation of hereditary differences. It also puts forth the idea of natural selection. In order to survive, the various living species must be adapted to the environment in which they find themselves. The more adapted individuals are more likely to survive and the less adapted less likely. With the passage of time, the better adapted increase in number, while the less well-adapted tend to disappear.

Genetic mutation and natural selection also combine to evolve species. For instance, sudden genetic changes work to bring forth species with characteristics that make them more adapted for survival. These characteristics become more and more varied by further adaptation. Thus from the mutations come individuals with favorable chracteristics that are inherited by their children, while those less adapted for survival disappear from the environment. Most changes are gradual and become obvious only over a long period of time.

This theory has made it possible to understand how animal species may be similar in some ways and very different in others in their adaptation to different environments. For example, what are fins in some species are wings in other species, and are paws in yet others. This theory sees everything progressing by evolution from the simplest living beings to humanity itself.

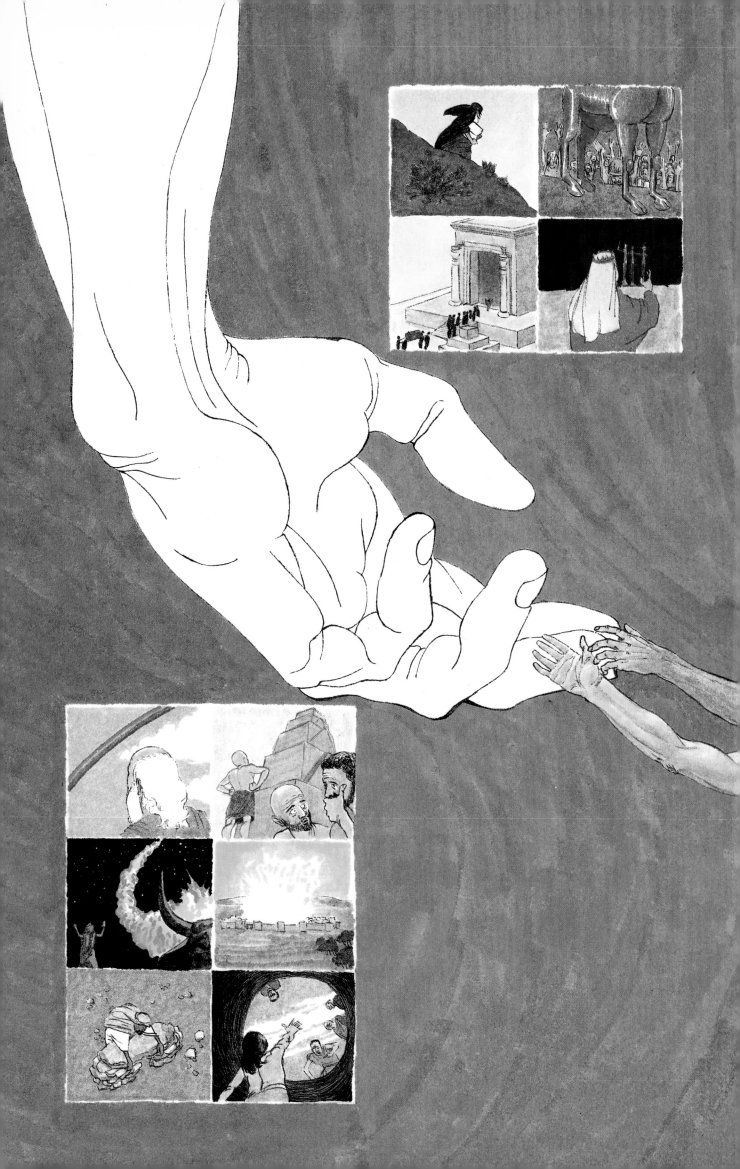

26 With the creation, God made
a covenant of friendship
with human beings.
With sin, humanity broke
the pact and rejected God.
The Bible and human history
show persons rejecting God
again and again
and God reaching out in mercy
again and again.

Most peoples throughout time have had an awareness that certain human behaviors are bad because they disrupt peaceful living among human beings. People also have had an idea that this way of living in harmony was established by a higher power, by God, who does not want the order to be broken. In these understandings, there is already some awareness of sin.

However, some peoples — for instance, the Babylonians and Egyptians — had a magical understanding of sin. They saw sin as an action that brings misfortune to the person who performs it. Accordingly, to free oneself from sin does not mean to repent of the evil committed; it means only to find a magical remedy, or cure, that will remove the danger of such misfortune.

The Bible clearly shows what sin really is. It is an act freely chosen by human will and knowingly committed without any concern for the will of God. Serious sin is a rejection of God's offering of love to human beings; it is the breaking of an agreement, a covenant, with God.

God's first covenant with humanity happened when God, acting freely, created the world and human beings. God wanted us as creatures to enjoy great closeness to our creator. At first, humanity accepted this plan and trusted in God's goodness. God and humanity lived in friendship. But then humanity's mistaken notion of its own greatness led to a break with God.

This is sin: the breaking of a personal friendship with God. This concept of sin is clearly stated in the later covenant at Sinai: God promised his people a land of their own and other blessings; the people promised allegiance to the only God, an allegiance that was to be shown by keeping the Ten Commandments. Israel frequently violated this pact and broke relations with God. The punishment of sin is separation from God. Sin is not only a personal choice against God, but a sickness infecting all human activity.

The Bible presents an entire series of persons in whose lives we can see the hand of God extended to establish a pact: to Noah, Abraham, Jacob, Moses, David, and others as well. The Bible is a history of covenants.

But the Bible is also a history of sins, a series of events in which humans rejected the hand extended by God: Cain slaying Abel, people living evil lives before the deluge, the construction of the tower of Babel, the evildoing in Sodom and Gomorrah, the sale of Joseph by his jealous brothers, the worship of the golden calf, the building by Solomon of shrines for idols, and many more — down to the time of Herod and Judas.

But God is stronger than the force of sin; God's mercy reaches out to the sinner and awaits a return, the moment when the sinner says, "I want to go back to God!" Then God's forgiveness renews the friendship. Once more, love, trust, and hope can grow in the human heart.

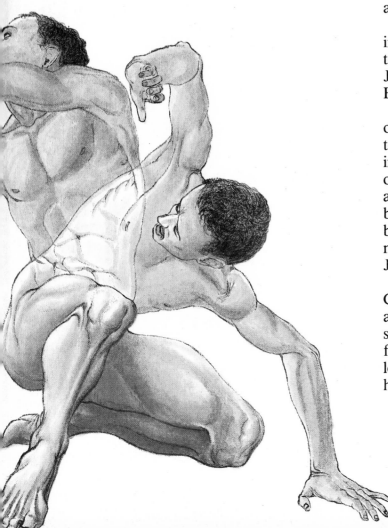

27 God created human beings
to live in love and fellowship
with their creator.
God loves humanity and invites
us freely to love in return.
God wants a relationship
with us that does not end
with death, that continues
in a New Creation.
In many ways God prepared
the world and human beings
for the coming of Jesus Christ,
the Savior.
In Jesus, the New Creation
has already begun.

The creation of the world and of human beings
is placed at the beginning of the Bible as the
opening part of a story of love, which turns into
a story of salvation. God made the world to exist for human beings, and created human beings to live in love and friendship with him.

Love, however, needs to be free; a person cannot be forced to love. So God's love is revealed
as an invitation to people, which, if accepted
becomes a covenant. In this way, the love is
mutual: God loves humanity and humanity
loves God. God's love raises human beings
from a purely human level and allows them to
enter into a mysterious life of communion with
God.

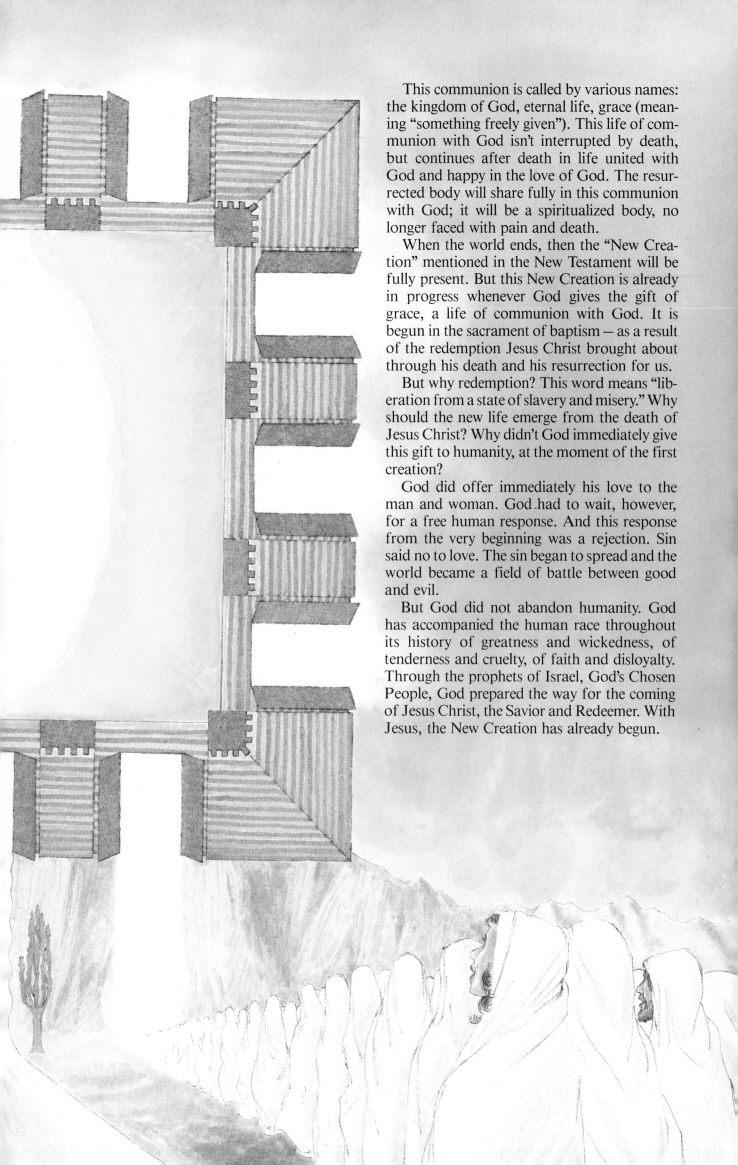

This communion is called by various names: the kingdom of God, eternal life, grace (meaning "something freely given"). This life of communion with God isn't interrupted by death, but continues after death in life united with God and happy in the love of God. The resurrected body will share fully in this communion with God; it will be a spiritualized body, no longer faced with pain and death.

When the world ends, then the "New Creation" mentioned in the New Testament will be fully present. But this New Creation is already in progress whenever God gives the gift of grace, a life of communion with God. It is begun in the sacrament of baptism — as a result of the redemption Jesus Christ brought about through his death and his resurrection for us.

But why redemption? This word means "liberation from a state of slavery and misery." Why should the new life emerge from the death of Jesus Christ? Why didn't God immediately give this gift to humanity, at the moment of the first creation?

God did offer immediately his love to the man and woman. God had to wait, however, for a free human response. And this response from the very beginning was a rejection. Sin said no to love. The sin began to spread and the world became a field of battle between good and evil.

But God did not abandon humanity. God has accompanied the human race throughout its history of greatness and wickedness, of tenderness and cruelty, of faith and disloyalty. Through the prophets of Israel, God's Chosen People, God prepared the way for the coming of Jesus Christ, the Savior and Redeemer. With Jesus, the New Creation has already begun.

Outline by Chapter

THE CREATION

CHAPTERS